Animals with Armor

Porcupines

by Julie Murray

Dash!
LEVELED READERS
An Imprint of Abdo Zoom • abdobooks.com

Dash!
LEVELED READERS

Level 1 – Beginning
Short and simple sentences with familiar words or patterns for children who are beginning to understand how letters and sounds go together.

Level 2 – Emerging
Longer words and sentences with more complex language patterns for readers who are practicing common words and letter sounds.

Level 3 – Transitional
More developed language and vocabulary for readers who are becoming more independent.

THIS BOOK CONTAINS RECYCLED MATERIALS

abdobooks.com

Published by Abdo Zoom, a division of ABDO, PO Box 398166, Minneapolis, Minnesota 55439. Copyright © 2022 by Abdo Consulting Group, Inc. International copyrights reserved in all countries. No part of this book may be reproduced in any form without written permission from the publisher. Dash!™ is a trademark and logo of Abdo Zoom.

Printed in the United States of America, North Mankato, Minnesota.
102021
012022

Photo Credits: Alamy, iStock, Shuttertsock
Production Contributors: Kenny Abdo, Jennie Forsberg, Grace Hansen, John Hansen
Design Contributors: Candice Keimig, Neil Klinepier

Library of Congress Control Number: 2021940118

Publisher's Cataloging in Publication Data
Names: Murray, Julie, author.
Title: Porcupines / by Julie Murray
Description: Minneapolis, Minnesota : Abdo Zoom, 2022 | Series: Animals with armor | Includes online resources and index.
Identifiers: ISBN 9781098226602 (lib. bdg.) | ISBN 9781644946565 (pbk.) | ISBN 9781098227449 (ebook) | ISBN 9781098227869 (Read-to-Me ebook)
Subjects: LCSH: Porcupines--Juvenile literature. | Spines (Zoology)--Juvenile literature. | Armored animals--Juvenile literature. | Animal defenses--Juvenile literature. | Veterinary anatomy--Juvenile literature.
Classification: DDC 599.33--dc23

Table of Contents

Porcupines 4

More Facts 22

Glossary 23

Index 24

Online Resources 24

Porcupines

Porcupines live in many places around the world.

They are found in forests, grasslands, and deserts.

Porcupines are good climbers. Many live up in trees!

They eat seeds, berries, and plant parts. They also eat **bark**.

Porcupines are 2 to 3 feet (0.6 to 1 m) long. They weigh 20 to 60 pounds (9 to 27 kg).

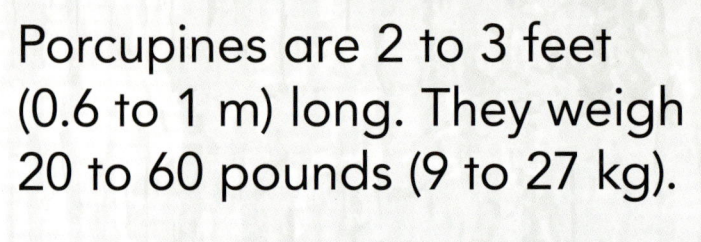

They have long, brown hair. The hair hides thousands of sharp **quills**.

The **quills** are long and pointy. They can have different colors and markings.

The **quills** lie flat on the porcupine's body. When in danger, the quills stand up.

The **quills** release when touched. They are painful! This armor keeps porcupines safe!

More Facts

- Porcupines are active at night. They rest during the day.

- They have about 30,000 **quills**. When one falls out, a new one grows.

- The only **species** found in the United States is the North American porcupine.

Glossary

bark – the outside cover of the trunks, branches, and roots of woody plants.

quill – one of the sharp hollow spines of a porcupine.

species – a group of living things that look alike and can have young together.

Index

climbing 8

food 11

habitat 5, 6, 8

hair 14

markings 16

protection 18, 21

quills 14, 16, 18, 21

size 12

Online Resources

Booklinks NONFICTION NETWORK
FREE! ONLINE NONFICTION RESOURCES

To learn more about porcupines, please visit **abdobooklinks.com** or scan this QR code. These links are routinely monitored and updated to provide the most current information available.